NonProphet Woke

The Reformation of a Modern-Day Disciple

Dawn Hill

Copyright © 2020 Dawn Hill

All rights reserved.

ISBN: 9781655537585

NonProphet Woke: The Reformation of a Modern-Day Disciple
Copyright © 2020 Dawn Hill Published by Kindle Direct
Publishing All rights reserved by the author. The author guarantees
all content is original without infringing upon the legal rights of
any other person or work. This book or parts thereof may not be
reproduced in any form, stored in a retrieval system, or transmitted
in any form by any means (electronic, mechanical, photocopy,
recording, or otherwise) without prior written permission of the
author, except as provided by the United States copyright law. All
Scripture references are taken from the Holy Bible, English
Standard Version (ESV), unless noted otherwise. Cover designed
by author. For World-Wide Distributi

If you abide in my word, you are truly my disciples, and you will know the truth, and the truth will set you free. John 8:31-32 Thank you, Jesus, for Your unfailing Word. Find me to be a faithful disciple and to walk in the truth according to Your Holy Scripture.

CONTENTS

Introduction

1 Twisted Scripture

2 The Upper Crust of the Church

3 Hoodwinked by the "Prophetic"

4 The Business of Ministry

5 Spiritual Abuse in Words and Warfare

Conclusion

Bibliography

INTRODUCTION

Titles. They sure do make us feel a certain way about ourselves. We seem to place a great deal of weight and significance upon them both in the world and in the church. Titles have their place and serve a purpose in these arenas. Titles help us to identify leadership. Titles are used appropriately and responsibly, and titles are abused. Though there is abuse present in both the world and the church, it does not change the fact that proper leadership is healthy and even necessary to maintain order and accountability.

For those in apostolic circles, you will find that titles and offices are of the upmost regard, particularly those calling themselves "apostles" and "prophets". Though it is stated from these pulpits that God is the appointer and anointer of the five-fold ministry, behind closed doors, a different narrative unfolds with unbiblical apostolic leaders. In one moment, you can go from a "prophet" to a "nobody", and in place of that office supposedly God ordained, those leaders demonstrate their "spiritual clout" by stripping said title and perceived identity away from an individual who is deemed a threat and dishonorable. That person is discarded with slanderous words designed to attack one's reputation and character. The one deemed a "prophet", "apostle", or whatever adjectives precede five-fold titles these days, is demoted and made an example to others who would dare question the hierarchy. The result of enduring such an ordeal is life altering. Some do not survive spiritually. In moments like these, you find out what will die so that God can truly be exalted.

I chose to title this book *NonProphet Woke* because that is what happened to someone I know. To those who had once prophesied over this person such weighty words of the five-fold that now seemed dependent upon their perceived heavy weight in the spirit, she was no longer worthy of being called a "prophet" because of perceived rebellion and dishonorable conduct according to the rules of man. What transpired in a matter of months was difficult and life changing, but it would be her emancipation from this abusive system. She became a disciple of Jesus Christ while embracing the NonProphet as she woke up from manipulation and deception.

Being woke is not as our current culture would define it, but it is a spiritual alertness and understanding of the truth. When this trying time occurred, her world was shaken, and she went searching for the truth. What better place to search than in the Word of God? The Word became what it has always been, the sword of the Spirit. It began dividing joint from marrow, soul from spirit and every thought and intention of her heart (Hebrews 4:12). The Holy Spirit confirmed what she had been discerning. There is a cutting the Word of God brings leaving no time for slumber. The truth brings pain and separation, and once you see the truth, you have a decision to make.

A price comes with knowing the truth and recognizing when something is not pleasing to God and in line with His Word and the Holy Spirit. The price according to "ministry" standards is substantial, costing relationships and falsely perceived promotion. When this happens, the sleeper awakens, and reformation comes. The course is redirected, and instead of going off the cliff, the sheep hear

His voice and follows Christ. Some of you reading this know exactly what that means. The one thing I can say for this particular situation is that in spite of the pain, heartache and manipulation, God's mercy sustained her through the entire ongoing process from accusations to separation to healing. As she has stated privately, "The pain was worth it to truly gain Jesus Christ."

There is a high probability that the contents of this book may offend you and anger you. It may be eye opening and liberating. It may test you and what you believe to be certain, and once you are aware of these things, you will have to judge what is written here for yourself against the Word of God and see if what is presented is truth or a lie. It is quite possible I will lose relationships. Regardless of how you feel about me and what is in this book, I pray that it leads you back to the Truth, His Word and the inner witness of the Holy Spirit. As a disciple of Jesus Christ and a dwelling place for the Holy Spirit, I truly believe that there must be a reformation within the church once again. There is a purification and a cleansing for the people of God to demonstrate corporately and in one accord, which can only come through receiving the atonement of our sin through Jesus Christ. We cannot become clean of our own doing, but rather we demonstrate that we have been washed and regenerated by the Word without spot or blemish because of our Bridegroom, Jesus Christ (Ephesians 5:26). If we truly know Him, we are to put on Christ. We must be willing to ask ourselves the difficult questions on an individual level and on a corporate level as we witness things taking place in our midst that appear as good fruit on the surface, but upon deeper inspection, the fruit bears witness to a bad tree not originating from God. Reformation will bring division before proper unity among those who are truly grafted into the Vine.

We are seeing history repeat itself with regards to reformation as seduction, prestige and manipulation are enthroned in the church. Scandal is rampant in our time and the church is sadly in the throes of this, especially in leadership. The entitled titled are more feared and revered than God. Though we have the Word of God at our fingertips, we seem to be in another dark age when the Word is not read or properly understood by the "commoners" let alone the "spiritually elite". Instead, ministers in pulpits are becoming the valuable commodity, instructing the flock of God through their own written words or proclaimed prophetic words rather than the written Word. If the Word is ministered, it is manipulated and used in an attempt to validate personal revelations contradicting the very God breathed Scripture that is our final authority. Paul prophesied that people would turn from the truth to follow myths. It is happening now. Congregations are being offered another Jesus and we are not taking the time to test the spirits and to search the Scriptures for ourselves. This has hit close to home and has been a difficult lesson, but an invaluable one. Thanks be to God for His mercy and His grace.

Prophetic ministry and emotional preaching are becoming superior to all else and to question a man or a woman held in high regards is borderline blasphemous. Personal prophetic words that exalt an individual are indulged as a way to draw closer to personal destiny and ego inflation rather than a call to die to self and to live for Christ. People are encouraged to fill journals with prophetic words spoken over them by prominent leaders and to empty their wallets and checkbooks in conferences and services so that God can do something in their lives. We are cryptically told that God's hands are tied unless we do something.

We are told to not put God in a box and yet, we put Him in a mason jar while we control the lid. Spiritual warfare and demonic spirits have their own books dedicated to their influence, a lucrative endeavor if you write about such topics. Yet the narrow way to eternal life and the judgment seat of Christ are rarely uttered in corporate gatherings, let alone written about in retail books. I know that this word will garner opponents and those who think that I am embittered and in need of understanding the mercies of God, but I believe that we are seeing God's mercy manifest in the midst of wickedness and carnal passions running rampant in the body of Christ. Paul plainly lays out in the Word a laundry list of fleshly manners that will hinder one from inheriting the Kingdom of God (Galatians 5:19-21). This passage is a warning from Paul to the church in Galatia. He is not speaking to unbelievers, but to professed believers and reminding them of the upward call to walk in the Spirit and not in the flesh.

The tough questions that we must ask are, if someone says that they are a Christian, where is the fruit to demonstrate that they are following Christ? Are they truly a Christian, or is it only in name? Who are leaders trying to exalt? Are they making duplicates of themselves or disciples of Christ? Where is the call to work out our own salvation with fear and trembling (Philippians 2:12)? This is not to condemn, but to wake us. If I say nothing, then I am complicit in this deception.

Truth be told, I grieve for the church in this and I desire

for the bride to know the Bridegroom in such a way that nothing in this world can entice her to deny His call to holiness and to true intimacy with Him. We must be ready for His return! There is a holy fear that those who think they know Christ without dying to self are deceived. The title Christian means little in this day unless you have been truly transformed by the redemption and atonement of Jesus Christ evident in one's life. We are called to be disciples, an adherent to the conduct to which we are called. Reformation is for those who will boldly rise up to declare the truth of the Word of God in the power of the Holy Spirit and the fierce love of the Father. This book is for those who will stand in the midst of persecution, no matter the cost. This is for those who are tired of another gospel declaring another Christ who cannot save. This is for the sober sheep who hear His voice and follow Him, refusing to listen to a stranger (John 10:4-5). This is for those NonProphets and every other man and woman who has endured spiritual abuse from wolves in sheep's clothing driven by fame, greed and control. If this book helps one person to come out of deception and into the truth, then it is worth it.

This book is not an assault on individuals, but rather the system infecting the body of Christ like cancer. We are not called to judge the world, though what transpires in this hour is disturbing and heartbreaking. However, we are called to judge righteously within the church (2 Corinthians 5:12). We are called to test the spirits as instructed in 1 John 4. We are to know those who labor among us and to discern rightly, and we are to mark those who would bring division and offenses contrary to the doctrine we have learned, and we are to avoid them (Romans 16:17).

We are to show ourselves approved and to rightly divide the Word of God (2 Timothy 2:15). We are to examine ourselves and to test ourselves to see if we are in the faith and if Jesus Christ is truly within us (2 Corinthians 13:5).

May this book not be founded on being right, but about being in righteousness before God through Jesus Christ, testifying of Him by the Holy Spirit. May it shed the light of Jesus Christ in areas where darkness is coming as light. May an alarm sound for those who will understand with proper discernment, and may we stay awake and alert, praying for those who are both led astray and leading others astray. May we be willing to ask God to search us personally and to test our hearts before raising the pitchforks and the torches on others. Consider this book a metaphorical way of nailing truths to the modern church door. May it divide the wheat from the tares. Let us be honest with God because nothing is hidden from Him.

For we cannot do anything against the truth, but only for the truth. For we are glad when we are weak and you are strong. Your restoration is what we pray for. 2 Corinthians 13:8-9

1 TWISTED SCRIPTURE

She physically jolted in her seat. Something had seemed wrong from the onset of this service, and she was troubled. This was the beginning of a set of meetings and while others seemed excited and in anticipation, she was restless. This was unusual because she had never felt this exact way before in this type of atmosphere. Now a moment of clarity came as she sat near the front of the sanctuary, taking in the offering message. Somehow the "apostle" had gone off on a ten-minute rant during this time about the proper ability of spiritual sons and daughters to listen and obey spiritual fathers. It had absolutely nothing to do with giving to God. It seemed prideful, arrogant and berating, but something else was wrong. These words came out of his mouth during his explanation of listening to spiritual fathers, "Jesus said, 'My sheep hear me, and they do what I say'. So, if you want to say that you are a spiritual son or a spiritual daughter...you've got to ask yourself, "Do you know how to listen?"" Her ears perked up as she heard the Word ministered incorrectly. The rant continued.

As the minister neared the end of this diatribe nestled into the offering message, the room was quiet as these words entered the room over the microphone, "Spiritual sons not only listen, but they obey...Jesus said, 'If you love me, you'll obey me. You will keep my commandments.' That is what the Gospel said." That is when the jolt came. It was a wakeup call to follow the Good Shepherd, Jesus Christ. She was heading off a cliff and the Holy Spirit was giving her discernment in this moment. This was a blatant twisting of Scripture to prove a point and to manipulate people into doing what they are told. That moment of clarity had her asking, "What am I sitting under spiritually?" She did not know at the time, but that was the beginning of the end for her as the "prophet" of the house.

(Note: https://www.youtube.com/watch?v=CG8T9KDrcLc, time 1:30:00)

****

The twisting of Scripture is a common occurrence. It would appear that the "proper" understanding of a particular passage of the Bible is insufficient without improper exegesis from superior leaders. Today the Bible is more of a garnish than the main course. It makes the meal offered appear valid as something upscale, but no one ever eats the garnish because it is not palatable. It is there for appearances only and left on the plate. The Scriptural verse referenced above was taken out of its rightful context in an attempt to validate a manipulative and controlling doctrine, which is something we will discuss in Chapter 2. In order to understand the Bible and the nature of God, we must have proper understanding in the proper context. This comes from simply taking time to read the Bible for ourselves and testing what we are being taught.

Take for example the plucked passage from the above account. The verse mentioned is John 14:15. Prior to this verse in Chapter 13, we see that Jesus is with His disciples before His crucifixion. In this chapter, Jesus washes the feet of His disciples, reveals His betrayer and gives them a new commandment to love one another. He also prophesies of Peter's denial of Him. As He continues to reveal Himself as the way, the truth and the life in Chapter

14, we come to the aforementioned verse, "If you love me, you will keep my commandments." Jesus said this right before He promises the Holy Spirit to them. The unmistakable meaning of the passage is that obedience to Christ's commandments is both a sign and a test of our love for Him.[1] The commands of Jesus are in reference to all of His teachings and His words. To obey His teachings and words is to obey the words of the Father since the Father and the Son are One.

John 14:15 has nothing to do with obeying church leaders or spiritual fathers any more than Jesus saying "My sheep hear me, and they do what I say" has to do with listening to spiritual fathers. In fact, Jesus did not say that, but He said, "My sheep hear my voice, and I know them, and they follow me (John 10:27). Again, the twisting of Scripture is to manipulate people into submission. To equate John 14:15 with obeying leaders and spiritual fathers is equating oneself with Jesus Christ, which is Luciferian in nature. This example is an abuse of Scripture, and it is irreverent to God. As disciples of Jesus Christ, we are tasked with testing what we are taught against the Word of God in its proper context. When we believe teachings like this, we are being led astray and conditioned to fear man instead of God. This is simply one of many instances where Scripture is twisted to mean something it never meant.

In my own personal study of the Bible and things which I had been taught through the years, I sadly found other passages that seemed to be misrepresented and in my lack of due diligence to study the Word, I blindly believed the teachings. I never questioned it, believing that others knew what they were teaching. It was spiritual laziness on my part. One example that comes to mind is John 10:10, "The thief comes only to steal, kill and destroy. I came that they may have life and have it abundantly." These are the words of Jesus Christ. Many have been told or have been led to believe that the thief here is Satan. We like to quote this during a passionate sermon about the devil and our promise of the abundant life in our understanding of abundance and prosperity.

However, when you read this passage in the proper context, you will quickly realize that Jesus is referencing false teachers as thieves and their lack of care for the flock in their robbery of the truth. He contrasts what the Pharisees and false teachers have done to the people to Himself as the Good Shepherd. Jesus has come to give eternal life. That is the abundant life to which He is speaking. Another point here is that this is not a guarantee of material abundance, but spiritual abundance that is only found in Christ. This error may not sound like a big deal to some, but it is a big deal when you believe parts of the Bible to mean something which they do not mean, and it begs the question, "Am I truly following Christ?"

Another example in the Bible that is taken out of context involves two passages of Scripture. One is Proverbs 18:21, "Death and life are in the power of the tongue, and those who love it will eat its fruits and Proverbs 23:7, "For as he thinks in his heart, so is he." NKJV I was taught to declare things and to watch what I said because I was speaking things into existence. These passages are twisted to justify this teaching. Yet this in no way implies that we create things with our words. God creates and He alone creates. We are not little gods with creative power. We can encourage or discourage with our words and our tongue can be a world of unrighteousness

(James 3:6). But we cannot create things or call things into existence. If that were so, then why would we need a Savior when we are already playing God? We are called to prayer and to seek God in all things. We are told to have faith in God, not faith in our faith. If we are going to quote Scripture, then we need to know what it truly says. In addition, that part of Proverbs 23:7 is not the full text but a portion. The full verse says in the New King James, "For as he thinks in his heart, so is he. "Eat and drink!" he says to you, but his heart is not with you." When in the proper context, we can see yet again that the meaning changes. Other passages could be mentioned and explained that have been misrepresented, but the point is that we need to be studying the Word of God for ourselves and making sure that what we are spiritually eating is truth and leading us back to Jesus Christ.

The Bible is about Jesus Christ

There is a simple realization that we must come to understand as a Christian if we are to mature in our relationship with God. It is offensive and much needed because the course is being offset by not understanding the truth. When I woke up spiritually and realized this, it brought much repentance and a desire to read the Word of God even more. Here it is, the Bible is not about us. We are not the focus. We are not the center. It is not our blood that runs like a scarlet thread through the pages of the Holy Spirit inspired words penned by men to testify of Jesus Christ. From the Old Testament to the New Testament, Jesus is throughout the Bible. Stories of men and women allude to Him. Prophets spoke of Him hundreds of years before He came in the flesh as all man and all God. Disciples gave their lives to testify of Him and the relationship they had with Him in life and the relationship they would have with Him in eternity. This Book is about Him.

It is interesting and sad that many do not read the Bible except for a few minutes on Sunday mornings in a corporate gathering. Maybe the Bible is not read at all. Maybe it is taken out of context to suit our notions and to make us the savior or the hero. Jesus Christ is the only Savior. You cannot know Him without knowing the Word of God. You cannot know what grieves the Holy Spirit and the heart of the Father without knowing this Word. This is the true prophetic Word, the testimony of Jesus. If we become the center of the Bible and the focus within the words, where does that leave Jesus? Saints, I encourage you, read the Bible. Every day. Knowing the One who is the Word is vital, and you cannot fully know Him without knowing His Word. The Bible is Christ centered. Anything less is a different narration, and quite frankly, idolatry.

Back to the basics, back to the Gospel

In a recent study performed about Bible readership, over four thousand individuals 18 years old and up were surveyed between 2018 and 2019. Of those surveyed, 30-31% said that they never read the Bible. This was the highest percentage recorded. Those who read the Bible daily were 15-16%. [2] This should give us pause. Why are we not reading the Word of God more frequently? The written Word of God is the greatest prophetic writing you and I will ever read. It testifies of Jesus Christ. This is our way of understanding the true nature of God. We learn in the Word what God loves and what He hates. It gives clear understanding as to how we inherit the Kingdom of God, and it is not by what we do but by what He had already done. We receive instruction that is designed to produce good fruit in us as His disciples and to glorify God.

The issue comes in viewing the Bible as a boring and irrelevant book. It is a sad state of affairs when recycled prophetic words and mythical unbiblical teachings are held in more regard than the Bible. I will sound the alarm on this without apology: if we were to test what is being written or released to the masses against the Word of God, we would find that much is wood, hay and stubble. It is not biblically sound. We must get back to the foundation upon which we are to stand. This is the foundation of our intimacy with God.

Psalm 40:8 says, "I delight to do your will, O my God; your law is within my heart." We know that the New Covenant has been established through Jesus Christ and His sacrifice and atonement for our sins. He is the Word, and He gave new commands, which fulfilled the Old Covenant: to love the Lord with all of our mind, soul and strength and to love our neighbor as ourselves. When we know the One who is the Word and we abide in Him, we can truly testify that His Word is written on our hearts of flesh. We demonstrate what Paul said to the Corinthian church, that we are a letter from Christ, written by the Spirit of the Living God on tablets of human hearts (2 Corinthians 3:3).

It is vital as professed believers in Jesus Christ and adopted sons of God that the Word of God, the infallible Word of God is the foundation upon which we base our relationship with God. Jesus Christ is our chief cornerstone, the sure foundation, the Word made flesh.

There should be a zeal and a desire for the Word of God in every true believer. David testified of this in Psalm 119:97 when he said, "Oh how I love your law! All day long it is my meditation." If we do not love the Word and we do not meditate on His Word, then we reject true intimacy with God. And when we meditate on His Word, this means not editing His Word, redacting what offends and separates the true from the false. Meditating on His Word will bring maturity in the body of Christ and will help us to not be deceived by winds of doctrine.

As God calls us into maturity, He desires for His bride to have a solid foundation upon the Word of God, worshiping the Lord in Spirit and in truth. Let me say this with all humility: our foundation cannot be found merely in prophetic words received through fallible vessels, but every word must be tested against Scripture. Intimacy with God is not assured in how many times we fall under the power of God or how many manifestations we attest to witness. Intimacy is not measured in accuracy of prophecy. It is not found in titles or accolades of man. Intimacy is evident in our testifying of Jesus Christ by His Spirit and by the Word of God and consummation is found in the fruits of the Spirit manifesting in our lives as the branches abiding in the Vine. Period. If you want to consummate fellowship with God, you must know His Word. How can we be doers of the Word when we do not even know what it says?

Fellow brothers and sisters in Christ, you and I have a responsibility to know the Word of God in its proper context. This is part of our personal relationship with God. Goosebumps and manifestations are not the plumb line of intimacy with God. You can have every manifestation imagined and yet not know Him or He even be amid those things. I believe that we are heading down a dangerous path when Scripture is not consulted in personal and corporate conduct. The Word of God is the plumb line and a testimony in our lives to how we truly know Christ. For all our talk of encountering God and seeking manifestations as true intimacy, we have become unstable, and we are believing things that are not the truth according to Scripture and to the witness of the Holy Spirit.

We must get back to ministering the Word of God unadulterated and without apology. We must return to the simple Gospel. Many are being seduced by doctrines of demons and by myths. We seem to think that the Word alone is not enough and that more power is required, but Paul told the Romans that the Gospel was the power of God for salvation to everyone who believes, the Jew first and then the Gentile. (Romans 1:16) Getting back to the basics is looked down upon and degraded by those who want more flash and more hype. But Jesus commissioned His disciples to preach the Gospel first and foremost before doing anything else. (Mark 16:15) Here is a suggestion: pay attention to what you are being taught. Take notes and study in your private time what you were taught. This is biblical to do and is instructed of us as believers. Sheep are discreet about what they eat. Discretion is used in the first bites of potential food. Anything not passing the test is discarded. The Word of God in proper context passes the test. Anything else is to be spit out and discarded.

Sola   Scriptura

During the time of the Protestant Reformation, sola scriptura became one of the areas championed by the reformers. Sola scriptura means that Scripture alone is authoritative for the faith and practice of the Christian. The Bible is complete, authoritative and true. ₃ As Christians, we are called to base our spiritual walk on the authority of the Bible alone. 2 Timothy 3:16 says, "All Scripture is God-breathed and is useful for teaching, rebuking, correcting and training in righteousness." Jesus Himself, before being handed over for crucifixion, prayed to the Father on behalf of His disciples, "Sanctify them in your truth, your word is truth." (John 17:17) Sola Scriptura is all-but-explicitly indicated in 1 Corinthians 4:6, where Paul warns not to go beyond "what is written".₄ Jesus rebuked the Pharisees and confirmed the prophecy of Isaiah against those who would "teach as doctrines the commandments of men", forsaking the written commands of God. (Mark 7:7-8) The Word of God provides instruction for us while the Holy Spirit guides us into all truth.

We find in Acts 17:11 that upon Paul and Silas releasing the word to the Bereans, these people received it with eagerness, examining the Scriptures daily to see if these things were so. Eagerness is great. The issue is that too many times we receive things with eagerness alone. The Bereans also searched the Scriptures and did not simply rely on their emotional state. The standard has not changed. Imagine if we studied the Word daily like the Bereans when we were presented with teaching in the church. We would likely find that a good portion of what we have been taught is fallible and in disagreement with the God-breathed Word. We cannot afford to esteem tradition over the written Word. Not all traditions are bad. Much like the time of the Protestant Reformation, some traditions are being offered to override the Bible. Traditions are problematic when they contradict Scripture. One of those traditions in the apostolic is eerily similar to the papal authority in that time. It is the teaching of a hierarchy in the church.

2 THE UPPER CRUST OF THE CHURCH

This was the second meeting with the "Apostle", the one she had known as her "spiritual father". The first meeting had been called eleven days prior by him and each meeting went three hours long. A million things were swirling in her mind as she meditated on the accusations made against her. Less than a month prior was when the jolt had occurred, the awakening to the truth. Now after this second meeting, it was clear her days there at her home church were numbered, but for how long, she did not know.

She sobbed on the way home as reality hit her. Eighteen years she had served this ministry and been faithful to the "vision". This was all she had ever known as far as church was concerned. She had sat through these meetings while listening to false allegations launched in her direction of opposition towards the "founder of the house" during the special set of services. She had been accused of dishonor and rebellion for going to the appointed leadership with concerns from the set of services. She was accused of nothing short of witchcraft when it was stated that the prophetic atmosphere of the house to which she belonged was "off" and that this was confirmed by the entourage accompanying him, including a fellow minister who was apparently attacked with sickness in their body while there. She was told something was wrong with her and that his entourage agreed. Though a few other dissenters were mentioned by name, she was the main threat pinpointed.

She was called dishonorable and rebellious for not only sharing a social media post from a fellow minister the "apostle" did not like but for responding to his comments on the post she had shared. Ironically, personal thoughts contrary to his were not permitted and needed governing, even though he had commented that he was "unnerved by those who felt the need to govern others and their flow." It had not gone unnoticed to her that shortly after the dialogue on social media, this "spiritual father" had coincidentally posted spiritual thoughts, thoughts seemingly directed at her such as warning others to beware of prophets without accountability becoming witches to manipulate others, declaring that a lack of submission to a leader is rebellion no matter how eloquent the words, and apparently asking the question to an imaginary person who could post well, blog and issue loads of rebukes what had they built.

She was accused of running people off by the droves from the local church. Yet in all her years there, this was the first time she had heard such a thing. She was told that nine out of ten apostles would not sit in a second meeting with her, even though he had called the meetings, and he expressed frustration that she would dare to ask him questions in the previous meeting. She was told in no uncertain terms that he did not have to answer her questions and though this ordeal was a waste of his precious time, he knew that he needed to handle it.

He threatened to bring in other high-ranking voices to remedy this situation, mentioning how he had counseled with them and this situation with her was uncommon and out of order. She was accused of trying to govern him, but he told her that he was a strong man and would not be governed. He stated that people were prophesying against him and binding him up along with fellow ministers he brought to that church. None of that was true. Much more was said, but at the end of this last meeting, she was sat down from any form of ministry in that church and she was given a choice. She had to decide if she was going to submit to the founder of the house and to a prophet of his choosing to evaluate her in determining what was wrong with her.

A letter was prepared in advance to give her upon her answer. He appeared gracious enough to allow time for her to pray about the terms, but he stated that the letter would be placed in a file and given to her after releasing her answer. Six weeks would pass after that meeting with her sitting in the church unable to serve in any capacity. Six weeks passed of her feeling like her world was caving in on her while being falsely accused of so much. Four of those six weeks involved physical symptoms of chest pains and heaviness brought on by the stress of the situation. But in six weeks, the weight would lift, and she would be emancipated in more ways than one. **

(Note: The details of these events are nonexaggerated and can be verified by means used to document these meetings as well as witnesses present during the meetings. Social media posts were also documented via hard copies.)

****

One of the most telling and humble Scriptures about the role of an apostle is found in 1 Corinthians 4. Paul addresses the Corinthian church, telling them of the state of the apostles and how they are last of all, sentenced to death, a spectacle to the world, to angels and to men. He calls himself and the other apostles fools for Christ's sake, weak and held without honor. They hunger and thirst, they are poorly dressed and without a home while working with their own hands. They bless when reviled. They endure when persecuted. They are the scum of the world. (1 Corinthians 4:9-13) This is puzzling because in our day and time, this is not the picture painted by those who called themselves "apostles".

A broad brush is used to manufacture a different landscape by those who see themselves as the upper crust of the church. This can easily be comparable to the papacy of Martin Luther's time. Priests, bishops and such were held in high esteem and still are. In fact, it was referred to as an apostolic succession tracing back to the apostle Peter. To them, their words seemed to override Scripture. Their revelations and teachings were the gospel. Questioning their authority was not permitted and would result in excommunication and even death.

While physical death is less likely a major threat in Western culture today against those who would question an "apostle", the threat of "excommunication" from the church and the reality of being ostracized for going against the grain is not out of the realm of possibilities. The whiff of questioning or disagreement of any kind directed toward apostolic leadership is unacceptable and punished. The account above is not uncommon. Sadly, this is a major abuse of power rather than healthy mentoring. Dave Hunt's words ring true today as they did years ago when he wrote about comparable papal abuse and the truth surrounding the apostles of Jesus Christ, "Christ told the apostles to make disciples through preaching the gospel…whatever commands and empowerment the apostles received from Christ were passed on to all who believed the gospel…all Christians are the successors of the apostles."[1]

Much of the apostolic teaching today is centered on submission and obeying the hierarchy established by those who call themselves "apostles". Honor and loyalty are a requirement in these circles. This is demonstrated in dissociating from those the "apostle" declares religious, bitter, rebellious or worse, plagued with demonization. Loyalty is seen in those who will minister the revelations of an "apostle", whether it be from his latest book or social media teachings. Looking the part and acting the part show a "deposit" of your spiritual father/mother. Similar hashtags and social media posts leave a trail of "spiritual DNA" leading straight back to the "apostle". Leadership and others in the church are subject to surveillance in this day and age via social media. I know an "apostle" who monitors and has other trusted ministers and lay people monitor the social media pages of church members and leaders.

Monitoring includes taking note of those sharing posts of other ministries more than posts pertaining to the "apostle's" ministry as well as any posts that are deemed dishonorable. Online services and conferences are not off limits to surveillance, and harsh reprimands are doled out to those who attend the services of those not in alignment with the "apostle". Such attendance is considered dishonorable. The sad thing is that those who believe they are part of the inner circle are subject to such treatment as well. No one is immune. The deception is in the call to honor, which is ultimately a call to idolize that minister. Many of these "apostles" speak of having smaller inner circles, comparing themselves to Christ and the Twelve. Those smaller inner circles contain a revolving door so to speak, positions filled and replaced by those who can be controlled while discarding those who no longer go with the flow. The reality is that they are not Jesus Christ nor ever will be. None of this behavior honors God and it is contrary to the nature of Christ.

An unbiblical hierarchy

Whether admitted or not, there are those who call themselves "apostles" that believe there is a hierarchy in the body of Christ, and they believe that as an "apostle", they are that hierarchy. They will use passages of Scripture such as Ephesians 4:11-12, 1 Corinthians 12:28 and Ephesians 2:20 to support that doctrine. They teach the five-fold government, which is a misnomer since the Scripture does not appear to call the five-fold a government. However, despite this mention of the five-fold, the teaching now seems to be centered on only the apostle and the prophet. Stick around the prayer lines long enough and you will struggle to hear anyone receive the call to a five-fold evangelist, teacher or pastor. But we seem to have an abundance of prophets and apostles. The hierarchy of the apostle could not be more obvious than in those who were once called "prophet" now seeming to graduate to "apostle" almost overnight.

According to this teaching, the "apostles" and "prophets" are the ones who have the most clout in the church, and if you do not listen to them, then you are missing God and you are either less spiritual or demonically influenced (we will discuss that later in Chapter 5). Pastors are told that they need a "covering" and that they need to come under an apostle in order to be relevant and to do anything substantial for the Kingdom of God. If you come out from under the covering, you are in danger of a curse. It is ironic that in all our mention of "apostles", we see the truth of apostleship not in the words of man, but in the Word of God. Apostles commissioned by Jesus Christ Himself were "eyewitnesses of his majesty" (2 Peter 1:16) The apostle Paul gave instructions for instating elders and deacons as leadership in the church, not apostles. (1 Timothy 3:1-7, 1 Timothy 3:8-13, Acts 6:2) In his epistles, Peter exhorts equals; he does not command subordinates: "The elders which are among you I exhort, who am also an elder." (1 Peter 5:1) [2] When looking at the early church, we find that they met in homes and were led by these elders. There was no hierarchy, locally or over a wider territory, which had to be obeyed because of title or office. [3] This includes the marketplace. Apostles are only Scripturally mentioned regarding the church.

Furthermore, we are seeing adjectives assigned to precede these titles, adding a perceived level of increased authority and honor. Examples are Master, Chief, Senior, Head, etc. Interestingly, the only titles which seem to precede those who wish to be endowed with greater honor in the Bible are those who are a danger to the body of Christ according to Jesus, Paul and Peter to name a few (i.e., super apostles, false prophets).

Paul addressed the issue of super apostles when writing the Corinthian church, "And what I do I will continue to do, in order to undermine the claim of those who would like to claim that in their boasted mission they work on the same terms as we do. For such men are false apostles, deceitful workmen, disguising themselves as apostles of Christ. And no wonder for even Satan disguises himself as an angel of light. So, it is no surprise if his servants, also, disguise themselves as servants of righteousness. Their end will correspond to their deeds." (2 Corinthians 11:12-15) Jesus praised the church in Ephesus for testing those who called themselves apostles and found them to be false. (Revelation 2:2)

The truth according to the Word of God is that there is not a hierarchy of apostleship. There are not "haves" and "have nots" in the body of Christ. We need not fear men and women. An interesting thing to note from the account at the beginning is the "apostle" referring to himself as a strong man that would not be governed. Ironically, there is a passage in Scripture speaking of binding a strong man in order to plunder his house. (Mark 3:27) Many in the Charismatic church interpret this as a demonic entity. Being a strong man does not seem like a claim one would want to make if this is in fact a demonic entity.

True apostles and prophets are not commissioned by man, but it would seem that they are, which brings us to another important observation. These titles are of high value to those who demand authority, and though they may say that God ordains these "offices", their actions demonstrate otherwise. I know of instances where individuals who were once distinguished as "apostle" or "prophet" by their head "apostle" were no longer called as such once falling out of the good graces of the "apostle". One example is someone receiving a letter summing up the reason for accusations of rebellion and dishonor and those named in the letter were addressed by their spiritual titles, everyone that is, except the one whose loyalty and integrity was called into question. If these titles are so easily taken away, then why should they be garnered any respect except for those ordained within the confines of Scripture?

Church mafia and gag orders

As mentioned before, in some of these "apostolic" circles you will find surveillance is done in order to keep tabs on individuals. In some instances, when an individual posts something on social media that is offensive to the "apostle" or threatens his teaching, there are repercussions from that. The repercussions not only come from the leader, but they also come from trusted confidants, or the inner circle. At times, you will see a gang up in the comments attacking the person posing a threat. Stronger in numbers seems to be the motto, and these "apostolic" inner circles represent more as mafia style than the true church. The "apostle" is treated as the godfather and is revered as this powerful force to be reckoned with while the followers defend and honor to the uttermost, deceiving and being deceived at the same time. If we take time to truly understand the Bible in the proper context, we would find that this conduct is not pleasing to the true Father, God. Being Spirit filled should bring conviction to a true follower of Christ if they were to say things echoing the sentiments of mafia style behavior.

Spiritual gag orders are given to people in the form of nondisclosure agreements or non-defamation clauses so that nothing considered disparaging can be said or shared about that minister or their ministry. Never mind that the Word says, "Blessed are you when others revile you and persecute you and utter all kinds of evil against you falsely on my account." (Matthew 5:11) Never mind that Paul rebuked the Corinthian church for not being able to settle their disputes without lawsuits (1 Corinthians 6:1). We are told to rejoice in the face of persecution. We are told to handle such matters within the church. We are not instructed to have an attorney draw up a legal document for self-preservation. If we are ministering the truth according to Scripture, there is no need for such a thing unless one is fearful that the truth which is hidden about them will be revealed and that truth will hurt their bottom line and their platform.

Untouchables deceived

An ongoing abuse in apostolic circles is the "touch not" doctrine. This comes from the passage found in 1 Chronicles 16:22 and Psalm 105:15, "Do not touch my anointed ones and do my prophets no harm." You hear this quoted by leaders in the upper crust of spiritual authority or by those who do not want their doctrine challenged. You find it in hashtags on social media, adding that extra flair of warning and impending judgment and doom to those who would "put their mouth" on a minister. It is a way to silence anyone who would dare question the elite and to intimidate those viewed with lesser anointing. But is this an accurate interpretation? A closer look at these passages will reveal it is not.

The verse in question is in reference to the kings and the prophets in the time of Israel. David sang this song after he entered Jerusalem with the ark of the covenant. He was giving thanks to God, recalling God's promises and protection over the people of Israel, which were the anointed ones, particularly the kings. Notice the word touch here. When you study this in its context, this means to do physical harm. This in no way means to verbally attack or to test questionable teaching. Furthermore, upon examination of the New Testament, we find this doctrine of the upper crust crumbling under the weighty truth of the anointing being given to all believers (1 John 2:20). It mentions nothing of levels of the anointing being given to believers. John 14:16 says that believers in Christ are given the gift of the Holy Spirit. 2 Corinthians 1:21-22 states that believers have been anointed by Christ. There is no mention of a particular class of believers being more anointed than the other. This is propaganda within apostolic circles to control and manipulate people from truly demonstrating a gift of the Spirit, discernment.

Leaders are not instructed to launch curses and threats at anyone let alone fellow brothers and sisters in Christ. Remember in the previous chapter about the power of your words. Why would a mature minister threaten another believer with curses if they are teaching that our words have the power to create? Is it double mindedness to teach that God is a good Father not inflicting harm to His children while issuing warnings of sickness and such against His children by those who believe that they are the anointed and less accountable in the church? This teaching has created a class of untouchables in the body of Christ. It is a smokescreen and illusion because no one is untouchable when it comes to judgment within the church.

Many are quick to quote Scripture and to say that we are not to judge, and that is true when it comes to issuing final judgment upon a person's salvation or eternal destination. We as Christians are not instructed to judge nonbelievers. However, we are to judge the fruit of a believer's life. If you and I profess Jesus Christ as our Lord and Savior, then we are under fruit inspection. Paul told the Corinthian church when dealing with sinful matters in the church, "But now I am writing to you not to associate with anyone who bears the name of brother if he is guilty of sexual immorality or greed, or is an idolater, reviler, drunkard, or swindler-not to even eat with such a one. For what have I do with judging outsiders? Is it not those inside the church who you are to judge? God judges those outside. Purge the evil person from among you." (1 Corinthian 5:11-12) John instructed believers to not believe every spirit but to test the spirits to see whether they are from God as in that time they were dealing with those who were denying the resurrection and the incarnation of Christ. (1 John 4:1)

If that were not enough, we are reminded when reading the letter from Paul to Timothy that all Scripture is breathed out by God and profitable for teaching, for reproof, for correction and for training in righteousness that the man of God may be competent, equipped for every good work. (2 Timothy 3:16) A minister is to rightly handle the word of truth and to show oneself to God as approved (2 Timothy 2:15) As believers in Christ, we are not above questioning or correction according to the Word of God. No one is more anointed than another and the anointing is given by God not to lord it over others we deem less than, but to properly identify us as belonging to God and to teach us the truth. John says, "But the anointing that you received from him abides in you, and you have no need that anyone should teach you. But as his anointing teaches you about everything, and is true, and is no lie- just as it has taught you, abide in Him." (1 John 2:27)

Paul missed the memo

How odd is it upon reading the Bible that Paul did not pull the "touch not" card as a true apostle of Jesus Christ? When addressing the super apostles that were coming against his ministry to the Corinthian church soliciting for notoriety and greed, he counters their boasting by providing an account of his sufferings as an apostle of Christ, saying, "Are they servants of Christ? I am a better one- I am talking like a madman- with far greater labors, far more imprisonments, with countless beatings, and often near death. Five times I received at the hands of the Jews the forty lashes less one. Three times I was beaten with rods. Once I was stoned. Three times I was shipwrecked; a night and a day I was adrift at sea; on frequent journey, in danger from rivers, danger from robbers, danger from my own people danger from Gentiles, danger in the city, danger in the wilderness, danger at sea, danger from false brothers; in toil and hardship, through many a sleepless night, in hunger and thirst, often without food, in cold and exposure. And, apart from other things, there is the daily pressure on me of my anxiety for all the churches...if I must boast, I will boast of the things that show my weakness." (2 Corinthians 11:23-28,30) He goes on later to say, "For the sake of Christ, then, I am content with weaknesses, insults, hardships, persecutions, and calamities. For when I am weak, then I am strong." (2 Corinthians 12:30)

Where is this teaching among "apostles" and "prophets" today? Never once do you have an account of the apostles being persecuted and rebuking their persecutors with, "Do you not know that I am anointed? You better not touch me. You will be cursed if you do."

Never once did Jesus tell them to resist persecution and questioning. Why do we not know our history that eleven of the twelve apostles of Jesus Christ were martyred for their profession and preaching? The apostle John was the only one to die of natural causes, despite accounts of him being boiled in oil and surviving the ordeal.

You will not hear much of this teaching. Instead, what comes forth is a refusal to suffer and to serve and an open display of insecurity to be questioned out of fear of losing power and finances. Peter, Paul, Jude and James referred to themselves as bondservants. Peter referred to himself as a servant first and foremost, following with an apostle of Jesus Christ (2 Peter 1:1). When Paul wrote to Titus, he referred to himself as "a servant of God and an apostle of Jesus Christ (Titus 1:1). The true apostles of the Bible, the ones who laid the foundation along with the prophets with Christ Jesus as the chief cornerstone, demonstrated what cost was paid to preach the truth testifying of Christ. (Ephesians 2:20) A cornerstone is the first stone set in the construction of a foundation. All other stones will be set in reference to this stone, thus determining the position of the entire structure. 4 Jesus Christ determines the position of the entire structure so that the foundation already laid as written in the Scriptures by the apostles and prophets is sound. Many times, today when this passage is partially quoted, the focus is on man, leaving out the One who sets the position of the holy structure, the temple of the Lord. That One is Jesus Christ.

What of the prophets?

Despite the verse stating to "do prophets no harm", the prophets were harmed and killed. This statement was directed at kings encountering Israel as they wandered from nation to nation. However, the prophets were harmed by their own people since these men carried words of repentance and judgment due to Israel's continuous idolatry and spiritual infidelity and rebellion to God. Persecution was not reserved for prophets. On the flip side of things, I hear this at times and again, it is misused to create this higher level of spiritual class regarding prophets whether intentioned or unintentional.

Make no mistake, as a disciple of Jesus Christ, if you minister the truth of the Gospel of Jesus Christ, you will be persecuted and rejected. Jesus promised this would happen. He assured His disciples it would happen to them. (John 15:18) The famous chapter of faith found in Hebrews 11 ends with such testimonies. When this passage is taught, some typically stop at the first half of verse 35, "Women received back their dead by resurrection."

But that passage continues, "Some were tortured, refusing to accept release, so that they might rise again to a better life. Others suffered mocking and flogging, and even chains and imprisonment. They were stoned, they were sawn in two, they were killed with the sword. They went about in skins of sheep and goats, destitute, afflicted, mistreated-of whom the world was not worthy-wandering about in deserts and mountains, and in dens and caves of the earth." (Hebrews 11:35-38) These verses are speaking of those having faith in God while suffering. Some of these were prophets of the Old Testament. Isaiah was said to have been sawn in half. Paul testified to the church in Thessalonica that they were suffering the same things from their own countrymen as they did the Jews, who killed both the Lord Jesus and the prophets. (1 Thessalonians 2:15) Let us not forget John the Baptist who was beheaded. Authentic prophets knew that they would face persecution because of the message that they released and yet in spite of the persecution and threat of death, they ministered the Word of the Lord. It is my suspicion that if we knew the truth, we would have less people seeking to be called a prophet in a prayer line.

We cannot use Scripture ignorantly and improperly. We are all accountable and teachers of the Word will be held to a higher standard (James 3:1). Rather than threatening someone for putting their mouth on a minister, that minister should evaluate the teaching in question to see if it is sound doctrine according to Scripture. Whether we as Christians are facing legitimate persecution or false accusations, we are to demonstrate the marks of a true Christian: bless those who persecute; bless and do not curse them. (Romans 12:14) This goes for anyone, title or no title.

3 HOODWINKED BY THE "PROPHETIC"

A woman was called out of the congregation by a "prophet" to receive personal ministry. He had identified her by her vibrant hair color. As she went up for the prophetic word, he began telling her perceived things from her childhood and then he said something very interesting. He said to her, "I asked the Lord where the prophet was here and the Lord said, "It is the woman with the red hair."" The personal word continued with him saying to her that the Lord needed a mouthpiece. The mouthpiece seemed to be for that particular church. It was a heavy word for this precious woman to receive.

While this was taking place, another woman sat in the back of the sanctuary, listening to this transpire. She sat in disbelief at what she was hearing, and as she heard these words over the speakers, she turned to look at a fellow church member sitting nearby. They both had the same look on their faces, and they seemed to understand what was happening. The woman sitting in the back had been known as the prophet of the house. She was the one who a month prior had been accused of dishonor and rebellion. She was the one deemed responsible for the combative prophetic atmosphere in that house. She had been sat down and removed from public ministry under the "founder of the house". Shortly after the second meeting removing her, it was decided that the body there needed prophetic activation. A weekend of services was set up at the end of that month and this one was the final service to be "activated".

She could not help but notice a few oddly coincidental details to this prophetic word. The man administering this word knew this woman sitting in the back of the sanctuary, and he knew that she attended that church and her assigned title as a "prophet" in ministry. He was also known as a spiritual son to the "apostle". It was oddly coincidental that both women shared the same basic hair color. It was oddly coincidental that the "prophet" ministering had identified this other woman as the "prophet" there and that a mouthpiece was now needed in that church. A thought lurked in the back of her mind. Had there been a conversation behind closed doors to remove her from her position there? She had heard of the "apostle" speaking with other ministers in the past and having them do his dirty work when dealing with problematic people. She did not want to believe such a thing would happen, but it was glaringly obvious that a point was being made in this moment. She was no longer a "prophet". She was being replaced. The one who had made her a "prophet" apparently had the power not only to commission the call but to also take it away.

****

Prophetic ministry is a popular facet of ministry within the apostolic community. It is highly coveted and revered, and apparently "prophets" are heavily populating the body of Christ. "Prophets" are half of the hierarchy mentioned in Chapter 2. When I say this, I am referring to those who believe that "apostles" and "prophets" rule the roost in this hour and to question their authority is dangerous. Though I do believe that God can speak to us through dreams and such, the most accurate way God speaks to us is through His written Word. True prophecy testifies of Jesus Christ. This area of ministry is impossible to cover completely within the confines of these pages, and the goal here is not to debate the operation of the gifts. The focus here will be to address relevant concerns and abuses surrounding the theme of this book.

According to the Word of God, true prophets are identified as servants. A few examples can be found in 2 Kings 17:13, Amos 3:7, Jeremiah 26:5 and 7:25. [1] As noted in the previous chapter, true apostles had no qualms about identifying themselves as servants of God. This is to be the essence of authentic ministry, serving others for the glory of God. I have heard people get bent out of shape for not calling them by their appropriate title. Imagine how much more it would upset them to be called a servant, but that is what all believers are called to be for the glory of God.

Personal prophecy as well as corporate prophetic words are coveted in the church and held in high regard. If someone refers to themselves as a prophet, then they must be willing to have their words judged. The standard has not changed despite what others may tell you. True prophecy from the Lord lacks no fallibility. The Holy Spirit does not make mistakes. Paul felt it necessary to instruct the Corinthian church about proper protocol for prophecy, stating that prophecies needed to be submitted to the judgment of the church. As in the Old Testament, if a New Testament prophecy was contrary to sound doctrine, then the prophecy was to be rejected. [2] If we were to apply this standard to the prophecy given in the above account, that "prophet" should be held accountable for prophesying that word in a corporate setting, and that would have been done by the "prophet" humbly submitting those words to the leaders of the church for confirmation. Questions should have been appropriate to ask since there were coincidental factors at play. However, as we have seen in previous chapters, questioning is not tolerated by those in spiritually abusive positions. The issue compounds when the leaders are themselves compromised, leading to improper accountability or lack thereof.

Caution should be extended when speaking for God. This is not something to take lightly. We are warned in the Bible concerning false prophets. Peter compared false prophets and false teachers to one another as those who "will secretly bring in destructive heresies, even denying the Master who bought them, bringing upon themselves swift destruction." (2 Peter 2:1) The sad part to follow is that "many will follow their sensuality, and because of them the way of truth will be blasphemed. And in their greed, they will exploit you with false words." (2 Peter 2:2-3) This is a sobering passage to read. To know that the way of truth will be blasphemed by those who bring in things to the church unpleasing to God while cloaking it as something from God is disturbing. This is why we must be alert and know what the Word of God says in the proper context so that we are not led astray. An accurate prophetic word does not make one a prophet of God. Becoming enamored with an accurate "prophet" clouds discernment and could be leading people away from the True and Living God. Exploitation with false words can certainly include personal prophecy that is designed to transfer the wealth from the willing participant to the "prophet".

Many people seek out those with the title of "prophet"

these days to receive a word from the Lord. Many want direction for their lives, or they want to hear a declaration about their destiny. There is an abundance of words right now that are general in nature and very encouraging, but there is very little testing of these words, whether corporate or personal in nature. I have heard this passage quoted often in prophetic circles, "Do not quench the Spirit. Do not despise prophecies." (1 Thessalonians 5:19-20a) A period is put at the end of prophecies and what follows is ignored, "but test everything; hold fast what is good. Abstain from every form of evil." But test everything. In these prophetic circles, testing is frowned upon and viewed as judgmental and critical. But are we not disobeying Scripture when we choose not to test everything? When we do not test prophetic words, we set ourselves up to indulge in things that may lead us further away from Christ and closer to those golden calves, the "prophets". Saints, we need proper discernment so that we are not led astray.

Prophetic indulgences in our time

During the time of the Protestant Reformation, one of the major abuses carried out by the Catholic church was the use of indulgences. An indulgence can be defined as "remission of part or all of the temporal and especially purgatorial punishment that according to Roman Catholicism is due for sins whose eternal punishment has been remitted and whose guilt has been pardoned (as through the sacrament of reconciliation).[3] Indulgences were a large part of the Catholic church, and they were used to collect money from the masses. In exchange, deceased family members and even the surviving relative could supposedly diminish time in purgatory. In essence, indulgences were a way to get closer to God and to earn a thing through works rather than understanding that the righteous shall live by faith and that the only way to the Father is through faith in Jesus Christ. Indulgences funded much self-indulgence in the church during that time and corruption abounded. History has a way of repeating itself. The voices declaring truth were mocked and silenced in fear that power and money would be lost. But the Truth has a way of not ever being overcome by the darkness.

This was not only an abuse of power, but a manipulative maneuver concerning salvation and eternity. People were deceived into believing a lie while drawing them further and further away from the truth of the Word of God. In some ways, the charismatic church has their own prophetic indulgences that are leading people further away from the truth of the Word of God while blessing the "prophets". We have lost sight of eternity. We want blessings now. We want a beautiful destiny to fulfill without trial or tribulation hitching itself to us. We have told people to find the gold in people and to ignore the dirt. We are not to call out the negative, but the opposite of what we see. This is a forsaking of the call to repentance and to die to self. There has been much repentance on my part for the deception that I believed. It does not mean that we tear down people. It simply means that we truly understand what the truth is so that we and others are set free by the truth.

Prophetic indulgences are being offered to the self-established hierarchy in the Charismatic church and other parts of the body. It seems oddly coincidental that leadership and other familiar ministers attending a special corporate gathering receive the most prophetic words of anyone. Many want a prophetic word and inadvertently offer up monetary offerings in exchange for such a word or emotional preaching that offers no conviction before God. These words exalt man and not God, but there is a deception that these words prove favor found with God. The more money given, the more blessings will abound. At least, that is the promise. Never mind that we are promised being hated for the sake of the Gospel and that we will suffer trials and tribulations, but to not fear and to trust in the Lord.

Many prophetic words are being doled out without accountability and proper discernment. Revelation 19:10 is misappropriated, "The testimony of Jesus is the spirit of prophecy." Instead of testifying of Christ, leaders are applying their own authority, deeming men and women with great talent and/or monetary assets to stand in places of prominence without true repentance and reconciliation back to God the Father if sin is in operation. There may even be a false sense of security that if one receives enough prophetic words of validation, then he or she is approved by God or will escape judgment and accountability. Indulgences during the Reformation gave a false sense of security concerning eternity. My fear is that we are seeing a replay of this and it is causing a false sense of security concerning eternity because we trust these flattering words over our "destiny" more than the Word of God and the call to take up our crosses as disciples and follow Jesus. Many people are not having their "mail read". They are merely receiving junk mail with their name on it and God's Name is said to be the return addressee.

It does not stop there with "prophetic indulgences". We see this in ministries offering phone numbers to call and receive a prophetic word from a "prophet". Love offerings are not required but are suggested after receiving such a word. There are even Facebook "prophets" who will give you a word and just so you do not miss out on a prophet's reward, they have their PayPal and Cash app link available for your convenience. If you do not give, some of those same people will say you are stingy and if you question a prophetic word, you have a critical spirit. The instruction in the Word to test everything is not accepted in these circles. How dare one question God's anointed vessel? We have already addressed that previously.

Others offer courses and sessions for a fee in order to be "activated" to prophesy and to flow in other gifts such as healings and miracles. This is grieving to see. Nowhere in the Bible do we see people being activated in gifts. I know those who will quote a portion of 1 Corinthians 14:1, "earnestly desire the spiritual gifts, especially that you may prophesy." When read in the proper context, Paul was instructing the Corinthian church on the proper understanding of tongues and prophecy in church services. At no point did Paul tell them that earnestly desiring the gifts involved paying for them so that they could be activated. In fact, Paul lists the gifts of the Spirit in 1 Corinthians 12, and he tells the church, "All these are empowered by one and the same Spirit, who apportions to each one individually as he wills." It was not the will of the "prophet" that apportioned these gifts nor a payment for services rendered in these meetings. The Holy Spirit apportioned these gifts. They cannot be bought, and they cannot be forced into activation.

Paul also speaks of the gifts beginning in Romans 12:6-8 , "Having gifts that differ according to the grace given to us, let us use them: if prophecy, in proportion to our faith, if service, in our serving; the one who teaches, in his teaching; the one who exhorts, in his exhortation; the one who contributes, in generosity; the one who leads, with zeal; the one who does acts of mercy, with cheerfulness." Again, this states nothing of being activated or paying to receive the gifts. Later in 1 Corinthians 12, Paul questions the church as he concludes talking about the members of the body of Christ saying, "Are all apostles? Are all prophets? Are all teachers? Do all work miracles? Do all possess gifts of healing? Do all speak with tongues? Do all interpret? But earnestly desire the higher gifts." (1 Corinthians 12:29-30) It is understood that the answer to these rhetorical questions is no, not all possessed these gifts. All these listed are gifts, and the Holy Spirit allocates them. They are not for sale and they are not magically activated.

I am not saying that God cannot author a message to be delivered from one individual to another or to speak through dreams. God does as He pleases. However, the Bible is to be our main source of guidance in addition to the leading of the Holy Spirit, and the Holy Spirit will not contradict God's Holy Word. We are not to rely on "prophets", prophetic words, signs or omens in directing our lives. I have known people who were shipwrecked in their faith because of prophetic words that soon replaced God as their anchor. Words spoken over them did not come to pass, and they lost hope. You will hear "prophets" blame the individual for the failure of a word, but that is irresponsible. If a corporate word does not come to pass, then the body as a whole is blamed for not having enough faith while the "prophet" lacked for nothing. If the "prophet" lacked for nothing, then why was their faith alone not enough? Here is a comforting passage to help those who have feared the fallible words of man and who have been manipulated into submission, "When a prophet speaks in the name of the Lord, if the word does not come to pass or come true, that is a word that the Lord has not spoken; the prophet has spoken presumptuously. You need not be afraid of him." (Deuteronomy 18:22)

The greatest Prophet that we are to follow and to reverentially fear is Jesus Christ, and the greatest prophetic words you will ever hear or read will come from the written Word of God. Period. Here is a Scripture to ponder and to study, "Long ago, at many times and in many ways, God spoke to our fathers by the prophets, but in these last days he has spoken to us by his Son, whom he appointed the heir of all things, through whom also he created the world." (Hebrews 1:1) If someone proclaims to be a "prophet" or any other title and they lead you away from Scripture and God and further towards their revelations, they have led you to another "god". Come out from among them!

Spiritual wiretapping and pressure to perform

There is a well-known passage in 2 Kings 6 where Elisha informs the king of Israel about the plans of the king of Syria against them. The king of Syria was greatly troubled by this and suspected a defector among his own aiding Israel, but one of his servants informed him that "Elisha, the prophet who is in Israel, tells the king of Israel the words that you speak in your bedroom." (2 Kings 6:12) I have heard professing "prophets and leaders in the apostolic use this passage of Scripture to intimidate believers, warning them that their private conversations, emails and texts are not kept from the ears and the eyes of the "prophets". This is manipulation to the core. There are a few questions we should pose about this passage of Scripture to those who want to insinuate that they have a spiritual way of wiretapping into texts, emails and private conversations. Does this passage mean that Elisha was in the king's chamber? The servant does not clarify this to be the case. The Lord may have merely revealed these things to Elisha by His Spirit. This doctrine that "prophets" can hear private conversations and read private emails, and such is to be rejected. It is assigning a deifying power that is reserved only for God, and any accuracy coinciding with such a claim is to be tested as the demonic can also appear accurate. Again, accuracy is not the measure but rather the Holy Spirit testifying of Jesus Christ through the professing minister.

Another thing you will hear in these circles is that true prophets must demonstrate miracles and signs. Not only that but personal prophetic words are a staple in the ministry of a "prophet". If you are not flowing in miracles, signs and wonders, or if you do not give into the pressure to perform and to conjure up personal prophecy or extrabiblical revelation, you are looked down upon and are not considered a "prophet". Leaders will use examples such as Elijah and Elisha ad nauseam in order to prove their point and their meetings are bent toward personal prophecy, performing signs and regaling puffed up stories of self. However, there is a wrench in this doctrine. If all true prophets demonstrate signs and miracles, what do we do with John 10:41, "And many came to him (Jesus). And they said, "John did no sign, but everything that John said about this man was true. And many believed in him (Jesus) there."? John the Baptist did not perform signs or miracles. The power was in the message testifying of Jesus Christ. Yet we have "prophets" prophesying a John the Baptist generation to arise while stating that miracles, signs and wonders are mandatory in Spirit filled believers. Is anyone else seeing a contradiction here?

John testified and prepared the way for Jesus Christ as was prophesied of Him by Isaiah. (Isaiah 40:3) He did not prophesy with mystical verbiage or lofty personal prophecy. Rather, he called for repentance, a simple yet profound message that is the foundation for every follower of Jesus Christ. Yet many are clamoring for the next great revelation and perversely seeking signs and wonders, not realizing that the greatest miracle was found in the call to salvation from the wrath of God through the atoning blood of Jesus Christ, the Lamb who takes away the sins of the world. John did no sign, but the truth proclaimed about Christ resulted in the miracle of eternal life to those who would believe.

It is an interesting inconsistency to consider that in the hype and great emphasis regarding Elijah, Elisha and other prophets revered by the apostolic for miracles and such, those who speak out and sound the alarm in the church and identify error in this movement are ironically criticized for being too much like the Old Testament prophets in the Bible who issued "doom and gloom". They are said to be embittered and lacking grace and mercy. The current prophetic movement has been conditioned to say what is popular and attracts the masses. The fear of the Lord is absent. Ignore the dirt and call out the gold. Decree and declare extrabiblical revelation that is palatable. We would do well to meditate on the words God released through Jeremiah, "Do not listen to the words of the prophets who prophesy to you, filling you with vain hopes. They speak visions of their own minds, not from the mouth of the

Lord. They say continually to those who despise the word of the Lord, 'It shall be well with you'; and to everyone who stubbornly follows his own heart, they say, 'No disaster shall come upon you.'" (Jeremiah 23:16-17)

God goes on to say through Jeremiah that he did not send the prophets, nor did He speak to them, yet they ran and prophesied. He rebukes them for declaring lying dreams to people and for causing people to forget God. If they had stood in His council, they would have called for repentance. (Jeremiah 23:21-27) Repentance is still for today and inspired preaching through the Word of God as the foundation and source is purely prophetic in nature. After all, the testimony of Jesus is the spirit of prophecy. (Revelation 19:10)

Chasing Dragonflies and lusting for signs

Currently there is a great draw toward signs in the apostolic/prophetic circles. People take great stock in them and allow them to help determine the course of their lives. These signs vary from names with particular meanings to specific objects or items manifesting and the repetitive appearance of numbers and such in moments of the day. Several years ago, I kept noticing dragonflies wherever I went. They would hover over me or my car. I had read from a "prophetic" minister that the presence of dragonflies symbolized transition. I also noticed many times that when I looked at the clock, elevens were prevalent, which was also said to be a symbol of transition. There are so many things that can be said to be a prophetic sign these days. I did not test these things or even read my Bible to see that this was neither a wise nor biblical practice. In my ignorance I participated, and I have repented since. A few months ago, while out of town, I saw dragonflies flying around me and suddenly realized that I no longer desired to chase dragonflies. I no longer cared about the numbers I saw or needing these things to decipher the course of my life. I wanted nothing to do with things that grieved the Holy Spirit. Doing such things is equivalent to reading omens, and the Bible explicitly states that this is not permitted. (Deuteronomy 18:10-12) This area may upset those who hold fast to this, but we must humbly consider this biblically, regardless of who teaches these beliefs or how popular they may be.

In Deuteronomy 18, God lays out commands for the people of Israel when they come into the Promised Land. He tells them that they "shall not learn to follow the abominable practices of those nations." (Deuteronomy 18:9) He goes on to tell them what these forbidden practices are, "There shall not be found among you anyone who burns his son or his daughter as an offering, anyone who practices divination or tells fortunes or interprets omens, or a sorcerer or a charmer or a medium or a necromancer or one who inquires of the dead." (Deuteronomy 18:10-11) The Lord had not allowed them to do such things. It was an abomination to the Lord. All these practices ultimately led away from God and to false gods, breaking the First Commandment. This commandment along with several others is fulfilled in one of Jesus' commandments to "love the Lord your God with all your heart and with all your soul and with all your mind." (Matthew 22:37) Interestingly, Jesus was referencing Deuteronomy 6:5. Sadly, the false god we are worshiping is self when we engage in such activity.

God has not changed His mind about such things.

Many Christians would easily say that things such as horoscopes, psychics, tarot cards and communicating with dead relatives are off limits. However, what about the "subtle" things that have crept into the church such as interpreting repetitive numbers in our daily lives or spotting a particular animal or object with an assigned meaning? What about the appearance of feathers in church services and in our homes? Do we dare question ministers who claim trips to heaven and conversations with deceased Bible figures? If any negative remarks are made against such things, then the religious spirit is said to be on the loose. But the problem is not in the remarks or the questioning. The problem is that we are interpreting omens and we do not even realize it. We are condoning necromancy within the church in the name of mysticism. We are doing something that is in opposition to the commands of God. We are lusting for signs and wonders rather than desiring God Himself, and we are not testing these things in a biblical way. Testing does not mean you are mean spirited, void of the Spirit or religious. Testing everything is biblical and instructed.

Fast forward in the Bible to the time of Christ and we will find the desire for signs among people who followed Jesus after He multiplied the loaves and fish (John 6), as well as among the Pharisees and Sadducees who questioned Jesus. Those in Jesus' day who wanted a sign were blind and deaf spiritually speaking. They could not see or hear the truth. They had seen signs directing them to the Messiah, but they wanted more.

People will say, "Well, what about the signs in the Old Testament and in the New Testament?" Yes, there were signs and wonders in the Bible, but every one of them testified of God as the True God, and the signs in the New Testament pointed to the Lamb of God, Jesus Christ. Those who desired a sign only wanted it for their own gain. Signs are not a guarantee of God's Presence. You can have every manifestation under the sun and not know Jesus Christ. The Bible warns us of false prophets in the last days who will manifest false signs and wonders with the ability to possibly deceive the elect. (Matthew 24:24) Signs are also not a guarantee that people will turn to God. John 12:37 tells us, "Though He (Jesus) had done so many signs before them, they still did not believe in him."

It is noteworthy to point out that Pharisees were known for adding traditions of men to the Scriptures and ultimately placing further burdens onto people that they could not fulfill. This was a major issue Jesus had with the religious leaders in that time. I would submit that the push for persistent signs and wonders in this way is placing burdens on Christians that is unnecessary and unbiblical by yoking them with extrabiblical traditions. Yes, chasing signs and manifestations can become a tradition. Can God do supernatural signs and wonders in the earth? Absolutely. Are we to chase after them? No. When evaluating the lives of the Apostles in the Bible, we find that signs accompanied ministry. They did not search for signs, but signs manifested to confirm God's omnipotence. Signs brought persecution and death threats both to the Apostles and to Jesus. Now teaching about signs and such brings notoriety and the elevation of man, and the signs mentioned today deal with things so vague that if you were to type them into an online search engine, you would have a spectrum of sites in the results from New Age and the occult to sites claiming biblical status with a heavy focus on angel ministry. This is a problem.

Let me state once again that I do believe the Holy Spirit speaks to believers, and God still heals, and miracles take place, real miracles that are beyond human comprehension and medical explanation. But when the revelation violates the commands of God and the boundaries of Scripture, it is to be rejected. Resist the urge to chase dragonflies. Follow God. The best way you can do that is to know what His Word says, and do not give into the idea that you must perform signs and wonders or have some outrageous revelation in order to be relevant in ministry. Our ministry is unto the Lord and not unto the "prophetic" relevance of the hour. Do you want to know your "destiny"? Read the Bible. It will tell you how you are to conduct yourself and who Christ is in you. Remember, the message of the Bible is Christ centered, not man centered Pray. Seek out trusted Godly counsel for major life decisions. All believers in Christ are led by the Spirit, and the Holy Spirit never gets lost.

51

4 THE BUSINESS OF MINISTRY

Did she just hear him say that? Maybe she misunderstood what he said. This was supposed to be a house of God, a part of the body representing Christ. But that was not the desired intent of the "apostle". He was disappointed and frustrated because the church there did not represent him well. He stated that people were funneled to that ministry because they bought his books and followed him on social media platforms. This area of his ministry seemed to be severely lacking in meeting this criterion. It did not properly model his DNA. Then came what she did not want to hear. The comparison of the church there to a well-known fast food franchise.

The chain referenced was known for selling chicken and for this church to not represent him well was like this dining establishment selling hamburgers in a given location rather than chicken. There were several mentions of businesses, including a remark to her personally that her behavior would not be tolerated by an employer. It was another wake-up call. She had ignored all the signs, but they were slapping her into reality. Though she was not part of the paid staff, she was still seen as an employee and she was expendable. She was no longer of any value to this "ministry".

The view was coming into focus. This was a business. It was not a ministry. It was not designed to glorify God's Kingdom, but the "apostle's" kingdom. There was no call to follow Christ. It was a franchise and this location in his estimation was floundering, serving hamburgers instead of apostolic network chicken, and frankly, she wanted no part of it.

** (Note: The details of these events are nonexaggerated and can be verified by means used to document these meetings as well as witnesses who were present.)

****

The call to ministry is a call to serve. When you look up the Greek word for ministry, you will find that the meaning is to serve. When we serve, it is first and foremost to God and then to people. There is a troubling trend in areas of the church, particularly the hierarchy apostolic/prophetic circles, to demand service rather than to serve. It appears as serving others, but there are ministries that serve the top of the pyramid where the man or woman of God is seated, cloaked in a façade called ministry. Others below them who buy the "product" can benefit from it, but they are kept in check so that they do not surpass the top tier. In reality, it is a business heavily focused on branding, advertising and self-promotion. This chapter is in no way attacking those who legitimately and sincerely serve God and the body of Christ while ministering and providing for their families. As the Scripture states, "The laborer deserves his wages." (1 Timothy 5:18) This passage is in reference to honoring elders who lead effectively and minister. Paul told the Corinthian church that the Lord commanded those who proclaim the gospel should ge their living by the gospel. (1 Corinthians 9:27) We must recognize that not everything calling itself ministry is such. There are wolves in sheep's clothing who in their greed are fleecing the flock.

Branding is a big thing in the business world, and it is a big thing in areas of the church world. Branding helps to set people apart and to identify them. It is not an evil thing, but a problem happens in the body of Christ when branding becomes more about being in man's image than in God's image. This was the heartbreaking aspect of the account above. It appears that the focus was on having that local church in his image and likeness rather than it being in existence to glorify Jesus. It is disturbing to know that there are professing ministers who feel that people are funneled to "their church" because of people following them on social media and purchasing their books. The church belongs to God. It does not belong to any man or woman. We were bought at a price, and that price is not a $14.99 paperback book nor is it being another number on someone's like or following on social media. I hope you are hearing this. Hired handlings are exposing the sheep to wolves.

The church is also not a franchise. People do not need to be looking for golden arches over the church. They need to be hearing the Word of God unadulterated. They need meat, not mystery meat. There is a lot of mystery meat circulating in church services so to speak. The church does not need this. We need to truly know Jesus Christ as our Lord and Savior and what it means to serve. The church is not a place where you can get it your way. God does not exist for us. We exist for Him. The business of ministry will focus on self and it will treat people as employees rather than fellow ministers. Profit is the name of the game. Networking is valuable for climbing the ladder to the top as well as financial gain, and if you have to knock others off on the way up then so be it.

Part of branding in "ministry" is the trend to post snide quotes or motivational thoughts that cater to flesh and emotion. I have seen posts of "ministers" claiming that God moved people out of their way so that they can climb higher, or that personal discernment for the "Judas" in your life is necessary. Really? This is rather narcissistic. Let's be clear. There was only one person who was betrayed by a "Judas" and that was the Messiah, Jesus Christ. The Bible prophesies that this would take place. In all sincerity, none of us have a "Judas". There is only one Savior. It is sad to me that things like this are posted in abundance by professing Christians with a prideful undertone, lacking honor to God or testifying of His nature. You will be lucky to find one shred of Scripture shared on their pages. The goal is to brand and to gain numbers, popularity and finances.

Green room talk

One aspect of the hierarchy is their need for "green rooms" in the church where guest ministers take refuge. It seems these rooms are for the inner circle only, and they seem to hold celebrity ministers and worship leaders. If you are asked to be an armor bearer, then you get to be in this room and converse with those present. I was in a green room one time with a minister I know along with several other people. It was after a service and while sitting in there, this minister and another visiting minister started talking about their wardrobe. There were several people in the room having conversations, but this one stood out to me. The particular topic was that of their red bottom shoes, which were very expensive. The minister I know began to tell of how he had left his red bottom shoes at a church and his assistant forgot to pack them in his suitcase. He had told the minister of that church to FedEx his shoes to him and to bubble wrap them, so they did not get messed up as they were very expensive. He then expressed his disappointment that the shoes were never sent, and he had to wait an entire month before ministering there again and retrieving his shoes.

The next night in the green room, having a captive audience, he regaled story after story of him healing people and ministering in power. I left that night sobbing on the way home and disgusted with "ministry". I have been in green rooms a few times, but nothing like this. It all seemed very self-serving. Christ was not exalted in any way. There is something that can happen in the life of a person when they come into money and notoriety. It may empower weaknesses in that person that were always present, or they may prove to be a faithful steward. The former is a repercussion from the business of ministry.

The price is right in apostolic networks

In 1 Corinthians 1:10, Paul writes to the church at Corinth and addresses the presence of division among the brethren. He asks for them all to agree and to be united in the same mind and same judgment. There were disputes taking place among the people in the church of who followed who. Some were saying that they followed Paul while others claimed Apollos or Cephas as their leader. Some claimed Christ as their leader. This was dividing the church and Paul reminded them that Christ is not divided and that He is their Savior.

While reading this passage, one cannot help but to see a correlation between then and now. In Charismatic circles, we find an abundance of apostolic and prophetic networks. These networks provide a "covering" and a "tribe" for those who join. While some of these networks seem to promote unity within the church, there is an allegiance established and understood to the founding "apostle" or "prophet". Any deviation from that brings division and potential expulsion. Instead of bringing the body of Christ closer in true unity, people are pitted against one another. It is a repeat of 1 Corinthians where those in a particular network declare, "I follow so and so." Some of these networks have become a breeding ground for cliques and divisiveness. We are not to follow a man, but we are to follow Christ.

Spiritual sonship is something of high value in some of these networks. It is a great honor to call a revered man or woman of God a spiritual father/mother, and it is an even greater honor when they call you a spiritual son or daughter. Paul referred to Timothy as his son on several occasions. Paul had mentored Timothy as a father would a son. However, we know from a previous chapter that this status as a son or daughter can be revoked quickly by the hierarchy. What is even more disturbing is that in some of these networks, you are called a son or daughter based on your level and frequency of financial giving. This is a demonstration of your honor and loyalty for that "apostle" or "prophet".

I have heard of such a network where this is the case. The top tier of the network requiring monthly giving will get you the title of a spiritual son or daughter. Unfortunately, that "apostle" checks with the overseer of the network as to who is a son or daughter as there are so many ministers who are part of his network. This is not true sonship. There is no reference in Scripture where Timothy had to pay his dues in order for Paul to drop the title "son".

Furthermore, Jesus said in Matthew 23:9, "Call no man your father on earth, for you have one Father, who is in heaven." This is in reference to the Jewish teachers who elevated themselves to titles of "master" or "teacher". These teachers ultimately sought to be called "father", seeing themselves as the source of truth rather than God. [1] It would appear that some of these networks are doing the same thing today. Though we respect and honor those who would spiritually mentor us, we should not have to pay a monthly due in order to be called an endearing title.

Ministerial shameful gain

The worship of mammon is a real thing in the business of ministry. In the Sermon on the Mount, Jesus taught about how we are to relate to material possessions saying, "Do not lay up for yourselves treasures on earth, where moth and rust destroy and where thieves break in and steal, but lay up for yourselves treasures in heaven...No one can serve two masters, for either he will hate the one and love the other, or he will be devoted to the one and despise the other. You cannot serve God and money." (Matthew 6:19-20,24)

Paul told Timothy, "But godliness with contentment is great gain, for we brought nothing into the world, and we cannot take anything out of the world. But if we have food and clothing, with these we will be content. But those who desire to be rich fall into temptation, into a snare, into many senseless and harmful desires that plunge people into ruin and destruction. For the love of money is the root of all kinds of evils. It is through this craving that some have wandered away from the faith and pierced themselves with many pangs." (1 Timothy 6:6-10) The issue lies not in having nice possessions but in those nice possessions possessing us.

Ministers are not immune to this, and some will do shameful things in order to gain not only in money but in prestige and honor. Some may manipulate Scripture in order to encourage financial giving. They may tell you that if you give a specific amount then God will answer your prayers and your needs more quickly. Some ministers may decide to preach to a specific race in the church so that they can access more financial gain and respect. I have heard of an "apostle" stating that he ministers in African American churches because of the money and their display of honor. To say such a thing is degrading and disrespectful and it begs the question that if this minister said such a thing, are his actions and declarations in favor of this community genuine, or is he using them for his personal gain?

There are teachings that have been around for decades, teachings that have deceived the church and drawn us away unto myths and greed, subtly calling us to be like God. This is not to condemn but to convict each and every one of us. I have repented of things I once believed to be the truth. It was not until I decided to search the Scriptures for myself and read books exposing the truth that I realized personal error and sin in these areas. This is an ongoing process for each of us.

It all goes back to using the Bible as a garnish for our

own purposes. When the Word of God is mishandled and not rightly divided, we see teachings such as the prosperity gospel, word of faith, the new apostolic reformation and so on. Names change but the purpose and the teaching does not change. Paul warned Timothy prophetically in 2 Timothy 4:3-4 when he said, "For the time is coming when people will not endure sound teaching, but having itching ears they will accumulate for themselves teachers to suit their own passions, and will turn away from listening to the truth and wander off in to myths. As for you, always be sober-minded, endure suffering, do the work of an evangelist, fulfill your ministry."

We can glean from Paul's sobering words. There are teachings that appease itching ears. Interestingly, this same passage was used against the Nonprophet in the letter sent to her accusing her of rebellion. This passage has nothing to do with rebellion, but she was labeled as rebellious for not listening to "sound doctrine" though none was presented to her. The absolute truth of this passage is difficult to hear. No one wants to hear the sound doctrine that they are a sinner deserving the wrath of God and that by His grace alone through faith alone in Christ alone are we saved from the wrath of God to the glory of God alone. No one wants to hear the sound doctrine that suffering is part of the Christian life as it was for Jesus. That does not sell books. There are ministers and publishing houses who know what brings in the finances, and they have fine crafted it into an art. While our ears are scratched to satisfy that itch, the coffer bell rings for those who desire to profit from myths and misinterpreted Scripture.

My prayer for those involved in actions like the ones mentioned is that they would be quick to repent to God and to be truly reconciled to the Father. This is grievous behavior that is hostile to the Kingdom of God and it is leading others astray. We are to represent Jesus Christ as true disciples of His Kingdom. We will not be perfect in doing so but thank God for His grace and mercy. Thank God for the Holy Spirit who leads us into all truth. We are servants of Christ. We are not CEO's of God's Kingdom Inc. Let's get back to our First Love and to ministry with sincerity and authenticity. Let's follow Christ!

5 SPIRITUAL ABUSE IN WORDS AND WARFARE

It was the day after Easter when she received the email. Six weeks had passed since the last meeting and since she was permitted to minister in the church. He had mentioned this letter to her previously and here it was. As she opened the email and read the contents, it became clear that she was being labeled as a defector. Relational and spiritual breach. Submit. Dishonor. Rebellion. These words stemming from a few months of accusations were appearing to sum up eighteen years in this ministry. She had been "removed from any form of public ministry within the church and all affiliated ministries until there could be a clear understanding of biblical protocol, submission and honor. The primary cause for the removal was rebellion." She did not understand. How was it rebellion to go to local leadership and express concerns one time? The letter went on to say that the "apostle" "deemed her unable to serve effectively in a ministry under his oversight, as long as there remained a deep and lasting disrespect, rebellion and disagreement." There was that word again, rebellion.

The pathway for restoration was delivered to her as followed: she must agree to personal ministry from a designated representative, appointed by the "apostle". This was to be a prophet of his choosing as he had stated in the previous meeting. Another stipulation in the meeting was an agreement on my part to submit to him as an apostle. From there this designated representative would report back to him with an evaluation, from which a decision would be made about her role in the local ministry. She was then provided with two pages of Scripture said to be regarding rebellion.

The letter seemed cold and disconnected. It also seemed contrived and very much like a template. There was one other detail that she noticed. Everyone mentioned in the letter was addressed by their five-fold title, everyone except her. It was a minor detail but one that seemed deliberate and calculated, trading one title for slander. It had also occurred to her that while her and her husband had both gone to leadership expressing some concerns, her husband was not removed from his ministry position at the church, but she was. This was the end.

After counseling with three ministers outside of the ministry, all of them advised the same thing after hearing all of the details from those few months: leave. A week later, she responded respectfully and with a blessing, stating that they felt it best to leave. On Mother's Day, they left peacefully and without incident. The Nonprophet was free. It would take time to understand everything and for God to heal her, but in the weeks and months to follow, she realized that getting out was the mercy of God. She discovered others had been maligned and mistreated by this "apostle" through the years, and she grieved for them and for those still deceived and manipulated by this "ministry".

**(Note: excerpts from the email referenced above were stated as written in the original document.)

****

There comes a time when we hear something so often that we begin to believe it. No matter what arena of life it may pertain, things taught or presented as fact enough times soon becomes a part of that person's belief system. Many marketing experts hold to the "Rule of 7" which suggests that consumers need to hear a message seven times before they will consider taking action. [1]

Repetition of a message can be a good thing or a bad thing even in the Christian church. A good thing is reading the Bible through many times and understanding the proper context of Scripture in order to mature as a disciple of Christ. A bad thing is when terms found or not entirely found in Scripture are repeated to masses of people so often that people soon believe doctrine that is nonexistent in the confines of Scripture. This can escalate to spiritual abuse by church leaders such as the one here. Several terms were repeated to create a false narrative of rebellion and dishonor. Witchcraft was insinuated by utilizing a well-known and abused passage regarding rebellion and witchcraft found in 1 Samuel 15:23. There are many words and spiritual concepts misconstrued and abused in the Charismatic church. Many times, we cannot see the abuse because we have fallen prey to the "Rule of 7" so to speak. We have believed what we have heard repetitively, and if we have never bothered to read the Bible and to search the Scriptures in our private time, we will find ourselves believing without question and we will be led into error.

I know firsthand because I was one of those who never questioned what I was taught. For almost two decades, I sat under teaching and absorbed it like a sponge. I read my Bible, but I did not study the Word and the teachings I was hearing. I read books that backed up what I was being taught, including books written by the church leader. When my leaders were attacked, I defended them without question. Because of that, I believed things that were abusive, reckless and unproven about others. Then a moment came when I began questioning some things, and when the questions came, the deconstruction began in more ways than one. But then a reconstruction and a reformation occurred, and I had no desire to return to what I had once followed. If you're still reading up until this point, I hope that you are willing to read further and to test what is said against Scripture. Let's rock the boat a bit with the spiritual abuse of words and belief regarding spiritual warfare that is lifted up as truth in the Charismatic church.

Buzz words and those with little press

There are certain words tossed around in the Charismatic community that see quite a bit of action. For instance, words such as rebellion, witchcraft and revival are buzz words among "apostolic" leaders. The latter is a positive buzz word while the former two are instated to those who are problematic. It matters not if they are truly in rebellion. Any hint of disrespect subjectively decided by the "apostle" is labeled rebellion and witchcraft. Witchcraft is a major buzz word in the Charismatic church, and this word is severely abused. It might make for a catchy social media post, but it is abusive and overrated. An example would be implying that someone operating as a "prophet" without accountability could become a witch using their gift to manipulate others. This generates likes and shares but is slanderous and void of truth. We would tend to think that since these words are so often used in the church they must be found in abundance in the Word of God. Let's find out.

When doing a simple word study in a Concordance, we can find that witchcraft is used only once in the New Testament. Depending upon the translation, witchcraft or sorcery is found in Galatians 5:20 as a work of the flesh. The Greek word for witchcraft here means "occult, sorcery, witchcraft, illicit pharmaceuticals, trance, magical incantation with drugs."[2] Witchcraft is only mentioned in the Old Testament five times (1 Samuel 15:23, 2 Chronicles 33:6, 2 Kings 9:22, Micah 5:12, Nahum 3:4). In 1 Samuel 15, the Hebrew word for witchcraft means "divination; This word described the cultic practice of foreign nations that was prohibited in Israel and considered a great sin." [3] The Hebrew word used in 2 Chronicles 33:6 refers to witches. The Hebrew word used in 2 Kings 9:22, Micah 5:12 and Nahum 3:4 means "magic, sorcery". [4] This is clearly speaking of those who practice such things that true believers in Christ would not do. Calling people witches in the church simply because they question teaching as the Bible instructs us to do is irresponsible and immature. Even the word rebellion is used a few times in the Old Testament. It is never used in the New Testament. Again, there are ministers who will downplay the relevance of the Old Testament in certain instances, but yet they will borrow passages such as 1 Samuel 15:23 to prove their point of rebellion and witchcraft.

This passage in its proper context is speaking of Saul rebelling against God, not man. We know this because the full verse includes these words of Samuel, "Because you have rejected the word of the Lord, he has also rejected you from being king." Saul would even rebel against God to the point of consulting with a witch and engaging in necromancy near the end of his reign. It seems that Samuel was not only rebuking Saul for his disregard for the instruction of the Lord, but he was in a sense prophesying of his future involvement with the witch of Endor, which was further rebellion against God.

Here is where the abuse runs rampant. Passages of Scripture are plucked out of context to manipulate and to control people. Another scary aspect to consider is that by taking a passage such as this out of the proper context of rebelling against God, a church leader places themselves on par with God by accusing others of rebelling against them. Obeying Godly leaders and submitting to them is biblical, but it is applicable to those who are watching over souls and as those who will have to give an account. (Hebrews 13:17) A Godly leader is not slandering other fellow believers with words to damage their reputation and malign their character. That is not watching over the souls of the flock. That is an attempt to spiritually kill a sheep. Church leaders of every title will have to give an account for how they have treated God's sheep.

It is interesting to point out that some of the most noted words in Scripture seem to get the least amount of attention compared to other words. The name of Jesus is used 981 times in the New Testament. The reference to flesh is mentioned 423 times in the Bible with 145 of those times being found in the New Testament. Sin is mentioned in the Bible 841 times. Repentance is mentioned 122 times. The term revival is not found in Scripture, but it is talked about quite often. However, there is little if any mention of a great falling away from God in the end times which is described in the Bible. (2 Thessalonians 2:3, Matthew 24:10-12)

It appears that we have an unhealthy emphasis in areas of the church when referencing particular words and malnourishment from not discussing others. In the Charismatic church, you will be hard pressed to find much teaching and preaching about sin, carnal desires and repentance. The devil or some other spirit is assigned responsibility for sinful actions while many are lacking accountability in this hour.

The reason I brought up the number of times the name of Jesus is found in the Bible is because it seems like we hear more about Jezebel or the devil than we do Jesus, which brings me to another point of consideration and possible contention.

Here a spirit, there a spirit

The demonic realm is real. When reading the Scriptures, we can see references to demons and to Satan. While on this earth, we are told in Ephesians 6 that believers wrestle not against flesh and blood but against demonic entities. We will face some attacks that are demonic in nature while on this earth while other attacks ultimately stem from being in a sinful and fallen world. People can certainly be possessed by a demon, and more so often than not, people are led by their sinful nature and carnal desires. However, there is an unhealthy emphasis on the demonic realm in areas of the church.

Some will hold to ministering and living as if there is a demon behind every blade of grass, every gust of wind and every human being for that matter. When applying this to an individual, there are teachings about many spirits said to be in operation, and there are people who get labeled with having a particular spirit. It happens frequently in the Charismatic church. Apparently, there are all kinds of spirits believers can entertain, some of which are not even mentioned in the boundaries of Scripture. I never paid much attention to it until recently when reading the Word of God, I could not find some of these spirits that have dozens of books dedicated to knowledge concerning them.

It is even more challenging finding the traits of these spirits in the Bible, but they are descriptively outlined in manuals and books by ministers. We need to be asking more questions about this because there is such a focus on spirits not found in the Bible and trying to combat them while assigning the titles of these spirits to those who oppose leaders in some way. There are entire doctrines being built upon the presence of these spirits. Is this biblical or are people being led off into myths?

The Bible does reference specific spirits just to name a few: familiar, unclean, evil, seducing, lying and antichrist spirit. There are references to such things as the spirit of jealousy, which would describe an emotional state. However, there are spirits presented to the masses that are not found in Scripture, and we need to evaluate this. It would seem that people have a hunger and thirst more for the demonic and the supernatural than for Jesus Christ, His Word and His righteousness.

The most common spirit in the apostolic/prophetic/Charismatic is the Jezebel spirit. Jezebel's name is mentioned in the Bible 23 times and of those, she is referenced once in the New Testament. There is never a mention of a Jezebel spirit, but somehow it is proof texted to imply that. I recently did a quick search on Amazon for books about the Jezebel spirit and 249 books popped up in the search. This is merely an example to show just how much emphasis is out there on this one "spirit".

Jezebel was a wicked woman who worshiped Baal and defied the True and Living God. Ministers teach that the Jezebel spirit is mentioned hundreds of years later in Revelation 2:20, but notice what Jesus says to the church in Thyatira, "But I have this against you, that you tolerate that woman Jezebel, who calls herself a prophetess and is teaching and seducing my servants to practice sexual immorality and to eat food sacrificed to idols." Jesus goes on to say that He gave her time to repent, but she refused and because of this, she along with those who commit adultery will be thrown onto a sickbed. Jesus refers to this particular Jezebel here as a woman, not a spirit. Somethings to think about here: How could Jesus give the spirit of a dead woman time to repent? Does this not go against basic biblical understanding? This may have been a woman named Jezebel in the church there, or she could have been acting similar to queen Jezebel from the time of the Old Testament.

Nevertheless, this is a prime example of creating teachings concerning this "spirit" because now with an abundance of teaching on the Jezebel spirit, we see more of a bend to label someone with a Jezebel spirit or to teach the church how to combat the Jezebel spirit or how to deal with people in the church who have a Jezebel spirit. The focus shifts from Jesus to Jezebel or whichever spirit is popular in that time.

In the Charismatic church, when people reference the Jezebel spirit and such, they are talking about demons. They are not speaking of an emotional way of conduct. Apparently, the Jezebel spirit along with several others are in multiple geographical locations at once. This puzzles me because I do not understand how this spirit or any other spirit other than the Holy Spirit can be omnipresent. This is equivalent to individual believers talking to Satan and rebuking him, unknowingly treating him as being omnipresent like God. How can demons be omnipresent? The answer is they cannot. When Jesus addressed Satan, He spoke to him in person. He did not speak into the spiritual ether around him while Satan was nowhere in sight. Satan is not God's antithetical equal. He is a creation of the Creator Jesus Christ.

Jezebel is one of many spirits that are mentioned by ministers in the Charismatic church. Others include Leviathan, python, Ahab, Absalom, Delilah, Judas, Saul, religious and orphan spirits. Several of these such as Jezebel, python and Leviathan are lumped together as water spirits. The reference to the "python" spirit comes from the account in Acts 16 with the girl possessed by the python spirit. The priestesses of Delphi worshiped the serpent there and took the name as such of being Pythian priestesses. The demon in this girl prophesied through her and Paul discerned it was not of God. This is a biblical example. Again, there is no mention of a leviathan spirit in operation nor a Jezebel spirit. Teachings about such things contradict and even overlap between spirits. How can one tell the difference if ministers cannot agree on the operation of these spirits that are said to share characteristics but is appearing to be conjecture?

This is extrabiblical teaching and is refutable. Furthermore, why are we assigning demonic spirits to dead people such as Ahab and Absalom? Other than Judas, there is no mention of their actions being driven by demonic possession. Flesh and sin are being taken out of the equation here. There is also a fabrication of spirits that are not even mentioned by name as a person. I have heard an "apostle" talk about how we are dealing with a peacock spirit in the body of Christ right now. Where is this in Scripture? It is not there, but it sounds good and it tickles ears. Again, I do not deny the demonic realm. I am merely calling into question our understanding of it and whether we are seeing great liberties taken to exploit this area of ministry with conjecture and speculation unfounded in the Word of God.

People are falsely accused of having these spirits for invalid reasons, and this should not be so. When people do not cooperate with leadership, they are assigned a spirit or label rather than addressing flesh, sin or the unwillingness to disregard the Word of God due to corrupt leadership and false teaching. We have been indoctrinated with things that are not biblically sound.

This is a common theme in this book to talk about the Bible and to be biblically sound. We do not hear that enough. We need to not only read the Word but believe it and obey it, and if we are taught something and it does not line up with Scripture, we can throw it out and reject it without concern of hurting feelings or offending others. An improper understanding brings spiritual sickness to where we do not even understand Christ as our Redeemer. We tell Christians that if they struggle, it is because they have a demon or a spirit. Where is this in Scripture? Would the

Holy Spirit share the temple with a demon in a blood bought believer, or are we denying accountability for sinful and fleshly behavior?

We are telling people that they must jump through all of these spiritual hoops so to speak in order to be whole. We are telling people that they must break generational curses when the truth is, Jesus redeemed us from the curse of the law by becoming a curse for us. (Galatians 3:13) The curse to the third and fourth generation fell under the law. (Exodus 20:5) His sacrifice was sufficient.

The truth is each and every one of us need to be in the Word of God. We need to spend time praying before God and really understanding what prayer is. We need to recognize that if we truly know Jesus Christ as our Lord and Savior then the Holy Spirit dwells within us. He is our Helper. He testifies of Christ. He convicts us and He strengthens us to walk in the ways of God. I mean no disrespect or ill will, but we have much goofiness going on in areas of the church, and this is one of them.

I do not want to spend my life chasing spirits that are nonexistent and trying to defeat Jezebel or whatever when the devil and every demon has already been defeated by Christ on the cross. We are to follow Christ. We will face trial and tribulation, but as believers we have great peace in knowing that Jesus has overcome the world, including the ruler of this world. (John 16:33) Those who truly know Christ and are indwelled by the Holy Spirit cannot be cohabited by the Third Person of the Trinity and a devil. We need not fear or look for the spirits of men and women that are dead and long gone. What we need to be doing is repenting of sin and having our minds renewed by the

Word of God. I fear that we "know" more about these "spirits" than we do about God.

For believers who are accused of being rebellious, religious or even a witch, ask God to search you and to try your thoughts and to see if there is any grievous way in you as David did so you can be led in the way everlasting. (Psalm 139:23-24)

James 4:7 is a well quoted passage and a sound place to end, "Submit yourselves therefore to God. Resist the devil, and he will flee from you." Before the devil flees, there must be submission to God. Submission to God includes His instruction laid out in His Word which will never pass away. This is vital. May we all grow in our understanding more and walk in the truth of His Word, and may we be willing to test everything and to abstain from every form of evil.

CONCLUSION

Hebrews 9:10 speaks of a time of reformation that was to come when Christ came and acted as the High Priest and the spotless Lamb of God who would atone for the sins of the world. The reformation He brought was a new covenant where sin was no longer covered by the blood of bulls and goats, but there was complete redemption because of Jesus Christ. The Holy Spirit would come and dwell within those who believe on Christ, and He would help them walk in all truth. The word reformation in the Greek here means "to straighten thoroughly, rectification, right arrangement, right order. It indicates a time when the imperfect, the inadequate would be superseded by a better order of things." [1] Another source stated that it means to "correct, amend the time of a new and better dispensation under the Messiah." [2]

We have much to be thankful for when we know Christ as our Lord and Savior. He brought the greatest reformation that we can ever know. He brought a right order and as the Messiah, He amended the time for a new and better dispensation. We are in a dispensation of grace and His grace empowers us to live holy and sanctified for Him. His reformation of eternal life is for the body of Christ as a whole and for us to come to maturity in Him so that we are not blown around by every wind of doctrine, by human cunning, by craftiness in deceitful schemes. (Ephesians 4:14)

If you made it this far, then you may have some

questions or some frustrations. I can relate. Keep asking questions and keep studying the Word of God to know what the truth is. Each of us must be humble enough to admit we have likely believed things that were not true. I can relate. Some will say, "Who are you to judge and to call out these things?" I am a Nonprophet, a reformed disciple of Jesus Christ, throwing out life preservers to those who may be drowning in deception. I climbed out of the raging water and after catching my breath from a painful ordeal, I clung to Christ and to His Word.

When reflecting on this, I am reminded of Ephesians 5:11-14, "Take no part in the unfruitful works of darkness, but instead expose them. For it is shameful event to speak of the things that they do in secret. But when anything is exposed by the light, it becomes visible, for anything that becomes visible is light." These things must be exposed. To ignore it is to be complicit, and I cannot remain silent while many are being spiritually abused and deceived.

Jesus said in John 7:24, "Do not judge by appearances, but judge with right judgment." The word judge here means "to separate, distinguish, discriminate between good and evil. In the New Testament, it is to form an opinion after separating and considering the particulars of a case."[3] If you are a believer in Christ, you are compelled to judge the fruit of this according to Scripture and the Holy Spirit. You are to judge this and to form an opinion after you have separated and considered the particulars of the case. This opinion is to be formed without bias or partiality.

Starting from ground zero

It is hard to fully convey all that I personally

experienced in a matter of three months. I was not the only one, and though that was a comfort, it was grieving. I experienced an array of emotions from grief and anger to feeling lost, alone and tossed aside. If I had not known Jesus Christ as my Lord and Savior, this would have destroyed me. His mercy comforted me, and His Word was a bedrock when all else was uncertain. When I felt nothing but pain and despair, He was there. When I felt disheartened and sickened by "ministry", He righted the course and showed me the way. I was brought low, but I now realize that it was necessary. He did not want me led astray, listening to the voice of a stranger. The Shepherd woke up this sheep, and every day the tears I now have are not of personal despair but of gratitude and thanksgiving. Thank God for this trial. Thank God it broke me. In the breaking came reformation and reconstruction. In the breaking came truth.

I realized that I needed to start at ground zero in my walk with God and make sure that the foundation I had believed was solid. The Word of God began to break things into pieces like a hammer. That sponge which had sat and absorbed everything for nearly twenty years was being wrung out. The Word of God is truly alive and active as I said in the beginning of this book. More questions came and the Word illuminated the straight and narrow path. That path does not restrict the Holy Spirit. God makes the path narrow for a reason. He sets the boundaries and the instruction for our good so that He is truly glorified.

As disciples of Christ, we are called to preach the gospel, the good news. Paul told Timothy to preach the word. The gospel of Jesus Christ can be summed up best here, "Now I would remind you, brothers, of the gospel I preached to you, which you received, in which you stand, and by which you are saved, if you hold fast to the world I preached to you-unless you believed in vain. For I delivered to you as of first importance what I also received: that Christ died for our sins in accordance with the Scriptures, that he was buried, that he was raised on the third day in accordance with the Scriptures." (1 Corinthians 15:1-4) We are to be a student of the Word and to minister the Word of God. We are to test everything, to hold to what is good and to abstain from every form of evil. (1 Thessalonians 5:21-22)

Jesus prayed this to the Father before He was betrayed and arrested, "The glory that you have given me I have given to them, that they may be one even as we are one, I in them and you in me, that they may become perfectly one, so that the world may know that you sent me and I them even as you loved me. Father, I desire that they also, whom you have given me, may be with me where I am, to see my glory that you have given me because you loved me before the foundation of the world." (John 17:22-24) The focus is on Him; the glory, the unity and eternal life given to those who will believe on Christ. Philippians 3:20 tells us of a great promise. After Paul speaks of those who are enemies of the cross, he goes on to say, "But our citizenship is in heaven, and from it we await a Savior, the Lord Jesus Christ, who will transform our lowly body to be like his glorious body, by the power that enables him even to subject all things to himself." This is our foundation as believers. This must be at ground zero in the life of every believer, above every personal prophecy and anything else. If this is not our foundation, then what structure is present will fall. This may sound simplistic and obvious, but there are many who profess Christ, but they are using other things as their foundation while trying to build. It will not stand.

As stated from the beginning, this book is not to attack but to expose and address things in order that others may have their eyes opened. My prayer is for God to extend mercy both to those in deception and deceiving others as He extended to me. I personally pray for eyes to see and ears to hear the truth according to the Word of God. Though anger may arise from spiritual abuse and deception among those who consider themselves elite, I remember the Bible tells us to be angry and to sin not. (Ephesians 4:26), and though I do not put myself on par with the Apostle Paul, his sentiments noted in 2 Corinthians 13: 9 resonate personally. Their restoration is what I pray for.

81

BIBLIOGRAPHY

Chapter 1- Twisted Scripture

1. What did Jesus mean when He said, "If you love me, keep my commandments?" Got Questions, https://gotquestions.org/if-you-love-me-keep-my-commandments.html. Accessed December 5, 2019.

2. Frequency of Bible reading among adults in the United States in 2018 and 2019. Statista, https://www.statista.com/statistics/299433/bible-readership-in-the-usa/. Accessed December 6, 2019.

3. What is sola scriptura? Got Questions, https://www.gotquestions.org/scriptura.html. Accessed December 5, 2019.

4. Ibid., Accessed December 5, 2019.

Chapter 2- The Upper Crust of the Church

1. Dave Hunt, *A Woman Rides the Beast: The Catholic Church and the last days* (Eugene, Oregon: Harvest House Publishers, 1994), 150-151.
2. Ibid., 149.
3. Ibid., 151.

Chapter 3- Hoodwinked by the "Prophetic"

1. David Freedman, *Eerdmans Dictionary of the Bible* (Grand Rapids, Michigan: William B. Eerdmans Publishing Company, 2000), 1189.
2. What is prophecy? Got Questions, https://www.gotquestions.org/prophecy-prophesy.html. Accessed December 11, 2019.
3. Indulgence. Merriam Webster, https://www.merriam-webster.com/dictionary/indulgence. Accessed December 11, 2019.

Chapter 4- The Business of Ministry

1. Did Jesus mean that we should never refer to our earthly father as "father"(Matthew23:9)?GotQuestions, https://www.gotquestions.org/father-Matthew -23-9.html. Accessed December 15, 2019.

Chapter 5- Spiritual Abuse in Words and Warfare

1. Jojarth, Marton. It's Not Nagging: Repetition is Effective Communication. LinkedIn, https://www.linkedin.com/pulse/its-nagging-repetition-effective-communication-marton-jojarth. Accessed December 19, 2019.
2. Spiros Zodhiates Th.D., *The Complete WordStudy Dictionary New Testament* (Chattanooga, Tennessee: AMG Publishers, 1992), 1438.
3. Spiros Zodhiates Th.D., *The Complete WordStudy Dictionary Old Testament* (Chattanooga, Tennessee: AMG Publishers, 2003), 1002.
4. Ibid., 530.

Conclusion

1. James Strong, LL.D., S.T.D., *The New Strong's Expanded Exhaustive Concordance of the Bible* (Nashville, Tennessee: Thomas Nelson Publisher, 2001), 710.
2. Spiros Zodhiates, New Testament, 471.
3. Ibid., 888.

ABOUT THE AUTHOR

Dawn Hill is a wife, mother and a disciple of Jesus Christ. She has a passion to minister the unadulterated Word of God and to see others come to Christ in Spirit and in truth.

Dawn is the writer and blogger known as the Lovesick Scribe. She resides in Virginia with her husband and her daughter.

You can find her blog at https://www.lovesickscribe.com